Book 1
Python Programming In A Day

BY SAM KEY

&

Book 2
C Programming Success in a Day

BY SAM KEY

&

Book 3
C Programming Professional Made Easy

BY SAM KEY

Book 1
Python Programming In A Day

BY SAM KEY

Beginners Power Guide To Learning Python Programming From Scratch

Programming Box Set #30: Python Programming in a Day & C Programming Success in a Day & C Programming Professional Made Easy

Table Of Contents

Introduction

I want to thank you and congratulate you for purchasing the book, "Python Programming in a Day: Beginners Power Guide To Learning Python Programming From Scratch".

This book contains proven steps and strategies on how you can program using Python in a day or less. It will contain basic information about the programming language. And let you familiarize with programming overall.

Python is one of the easiest and most versatile programming languages today. Also, it is a powerful programming language that is being used by expert developers on their complex computer programs. And its biggest edges against other programming languages are its elegant but simple syntax and readiness for rapid application development.

With python, you can create standalone programs with complex functionalities. In addition, you can combine it or use it as an extension language for programs that were created using other programming languages.

Anyway, this eBook will provide you with easy and understandable tutorial about python. It will only cover the basics of the programming language. On the other hand, the book is a good introduction to some basic concept of programming. It will be not too technical, and it is focused on teaching those who have little knowledge about the craft of developing programs.

By the way, take note that this tutorial will use python 3.4.2. Also, most of the things mentioned here are done in a computer running on Microsoft Windows.

Thanks again for purchasing this book. I hope you enjoy it!

Chapter 1: Getting Prepared

In developing python scripts or programs, you will need a text editor. It is recommended that you use Notepad++. It is a free and open source text editor that you can easily download and install from the internet. For you to have the latest version, go to this link: http://notepad-plus-plus.org/download/v6.6.9.html.

Once you install Notepad++ and you are ready to write python code lines, make sure that you take advantage of its syntax-highlighting feature. To do that, click on Language > P > Python. All python functions will be automatically highlighted when you set the Language to python. It will also highlight strings, numbers, etc. Also, if you save the file for the first time, the save dialog box will automatically set the file to have an extension of .py.

To be able to run your scripts, download and install python into your computer. The latest version, as of this writing, is 3.4.2. You can get python from this link: https://www.python.org/download.

And to be able to test run your python scripts in Notepad++, go to Run > Run... or press the F5 key. A small dialogue box will appear, and it will require you to provide the path for the compiler or a program that will execute your script. In this case, you will need to direct Notepad++ to the python executable located in the installation folder.

By default or if you did not change the installation path of python, it can be found on the root folder on the drive where your operating system is installed. If your operating system is on drive C of your computer, the python executable can be found on C:\Python34\python.exe. Paste that line on the dialogue box and add the following line: $(FULL_CURRENT_PATH). Separate the location of the python.exe and the line with a space, and enclosed the latter in double quotes. It should look like this:

C:\Python34\python.exe "$(FULL_CURRENT_PATH)"

Save this setting by pressing the Save button in the dialogue box. Another window will popup. It will ask you to name the setting and assign a shortcut key to it. Just name it python34 and set the shortcut key to F9. Press the OK button and close the dialogue box. With that setting, you can test run your program by just pressing the F9 key.

By the way, if the location you have set is wrong, the python executable will not run. So to make sure you got it right, go to python folder. And since you are already there, copy python.exe, and paste its shortcut on your desktop. You will need to access it later.

And you are all set. You can proceed on learning python now.

Chapter 2: Interactive Mode – Mathematical Operations

Before you develop multiple lines of code for a program, it will be best for you to start playing around with Python's interactive mode first. The interactive mode allows a developer to see immediate results of what he will code in his program. For new python users, it can help them familiarize themselves on python's basic functions, commands, and syntax.

To access the interactive mode, just open python.exe. If you followed the instructions in the previous chapter, its shortcut should be already on your desktop. Just open it and the python console will appear.

Once you open the python executable, a command console like window will appear. It will greet you with a short message that will tell you the version of python that you are using and some command that can provide you with various information about python. At the bottom of the message, you will the primary prompt (>>>). Beside that is the blinking cursor. In there, you can just type the functions or commands you want to use or execute. For starters, type credits and press Enter.

Mathematical Operations in Interactive Mode

You can actually use the interactive mode as a calculator. Try typing 1 + 1 and press Enter. Immediately after you press the Enter, the console provided you with the answer to the equation 1 + 1. And then it created a new line and the primary prompt is back.

In python, there are eight basic mathematical operations that you can execute. And they are:

- Addition = 1 + 1

- Subtraction = 1 – 1

- Multiplication = 1 * 1

- Division = 1 / 1

  In older versions of Python, if you divide integers and the division will result to a decimal, Python will only return an integer. For example, if you divide 3 by 2, you will get 1 as an answer. And if you divide 20 by 39, you will get a zero. Also, take note that the result is not rounded off. Python will just truncate all numbers after the decimal point.

  In case you want to get an accurate quotient with decimals, you must convert the integers into floating numbers. To do that, you can simply add a decimal point after the numbers.

- Floor Division = 1 // 1

  If you are dividing floating numbers and you just want to get the integer quotient or you do not want the decimals to be included, you can perform floor division instead. For example, floor dividing 5.1515 by 2.0 will give you a 2 as an integer quotient.

- Modulo = 1 % 1

  The modulo operator will allow you to get the remainder from a division from two numbers. For example, typing 5 % 2 will give you a result of 1 since 5 divided by two is 2 remainder 1.

- Negation = -1

  Adding a hyphen before a number will make it a negative number. You can perform double, triple, or multiple negations with this operator. For example, typing -23 will result into -23. Typing --23 will result into 23. Typing -----23 will result into -23.

- Absolute Value = abs(1)

When this is used to a number, the number will be converted to its absolute value or will be always positive. For example, abs (-41) will return 41.

Python calculates equation using the PEMDAS order, the order of operations that are taught in Basic Math, Geometry, and Algebra subjects in schools. By the way, PEMDAS stands for Parentheses, Exponents, Multiplication, Division, Addition, and Subtraction.

Chapter 3: Interactive Mode – Variables

During your Math subject when you were in grade or high school, your teacher might have taught you about variables. In Math, variables are letters that serve as containers for numbers of known and unknown value. In Python or any programming language, variables are important. They act as storage of values. And their presence makes the lives of developers easy.

However, unlike in school, variables in programming languages are flexible when it comes to their names and functions. In Python, variables can have names instead of a single letter. Also, they can also contain or represent text or strings.

Assigning Values to Variables

Assigning a value to a variable is easy in Python. You can just type the name of your variable, place an equal sign afterwards, and place the value you want to be contained or stored in the variable. For example:

```
>>> x = 151
```

When you assign a value in a variable, Python will not reply any message. Instead, it will just put your cursor on the next primary prompt. In the example, you have assigned the value 151 to the variable x. To check if it worked, type x on the console and press Enter. Python will respond with the value of the variable x.

Just like numbers, you can perform arithmetical operations with variable. For example, try typing x – 100 in the console and press Enter. Python will calculate the equation, and return the number 51 since 151 – 100 = 51. And of course, you can perform mathematical operations with multiple variables in one line.

By the way, in case that you did not define or assign a value to a new variable, Python will return an error if you use it. For example, if you try to subtract x with y, you will get an error that will say name 'y' is not defined. You received that message since you have not assigned anything to the variable y yet.

In addition, you can assign and change the value of a variable anytime. Also, the variable's value will not change if you do not assign anything to it. The variable and its value will stay in your program as long as you do not destroy it, delete it, or close the program.

To delete a variable, type del then the name of the variable. For example:

```
>>> del x
```

Once you try to access the variable again by typing its name and pressing Enter after you delete it, Python will return an error message saying that the variable is not defined.

Also, you can assign calculated values to a variable. For example:

```
>>> z = 1 + 4
```

If you type that, type z, and press Enter, Python will reply with 5. Variables are that easy to manipulate in Python.

You can also assign the value of one variable to another. Below is an example:

```
>>> y = 2
>>> z = y
```

The variable z's value will be changed to 2.

Chapter 4: Interactive Mode – Strings

Your program will not be all about numbers. Of course, you would want to add some text into it. In Python, you can do that by using strings. A string or string literal is a series of alphanumeric numbers or characters. A string can be a word or sentence. A lone character can be also considered as a string. To make your program display a string, you will need to use the print function. Below is an example on how to use it:

>>> print ("Dogs are cute.")

To display a string using the print function properly, you will need to enclose the string with parentheses and double quotations. Without the parentheses, you will receive a syntax error. Without the quotes, Python will think that you are trying to make it display a variable's value.

By the way, in older versions of Python, you can use print without the parentheses. However, in version 3 and newer, print was changed to as a function. Because of that, it will require parentheses.

For example:

>>> print ("Dogs")

That line will make Python print the word or string Dogs. On the other hand:

>>> print (Dogs)

That line will return a variable not defined error. With that being said, you can actually print or display the content of a variable. For example:

>>> x = 14

>>> print (x)

The print function will display the number 14 on the screen. By the way, you can also use single quotes or even triple single or double quotes. However, it is recommendable to use a single double for those who are just started in program development.

Assigning Strings to Variables

Assigning strings to variables is easy. And it is the same as assigning numbers to them. The only difference is that you will need to enclose the string value in double quotations or reverse commas as some developers call them. For example:

>>> stringvariable = "This is a string."

If you type stringvariable in the interactive mode console, it will display the This is a string text. On the other hand, if you do this:

>>> print (stringvariable)

Python will print the string, too.

Strings can include punctuation and symbols. However, there are some symbols or punctuations that can mess up your assignment and give you a syntax error. For example:

>>> samplestring = "And he said, "Hi.""

In this case, you will get a syntax error because the appearance of another double quote has appeared before the double quote that should be enclosing the string. Unfortunately, Python cannot recognize what you are trying to do here. Because of that, you need the by escaping the string literal.

To escape, you must place the escape character backslash (\) before the character that might produce conflict. In the example's case, the characters that might produce a syntax error are the two double quotes inside. Below is the fixed version of the previous paragraph:

>>> samplestring = "And he said, \"Hi.\""

Writing the string assignment like that will not produce an error. In case you print or type and enter the variable samplestring in the console, you will see the string that you want to appear, which is And he said, "Hi.".

Escape Sequences in Python

Not all characters are needed to be escaped. Due to that, the characters that you can escape or the number of escape sequences are limited. Also, escape sequences are not only for preventing syntax errors. They are also used to add special characters such as new line and carriage return to your strings. Below is a list of the escape sequences you can use in Python:

- \\ = Backslash (\)

- \" = Double quote (")

- \' = Single quote (')

- \b = Backspace

- \a = ASCII Bell

- \n = Linefeed

- \f = Formfeed

- \t = Horizontal Tab

- \r = Carriage Return

- \v = ASCII Vertical Tab

Preventing Escape Sequences to Work

There will be times that the string that you want to print or use might accidentally contain an escape sequence. Though, it is a bit rare since the backslash character is seldom used in everyday text. Nevertheless, it is still best that you know how to prevent it. Below is an example of an escape sequence that might produce undesirable results to your program:

>>> print ("C:\Windows\notepad.exe")

When Python processes that, you might encounter a problem when you use since the \n in the middle of the string will break the string. For you to visualize it better, below is the result:

>>> print ("C:\Windows\notepad.exe")

C:\Windows

otepad.exe

>>> _

To prevent that you must convert your string to a raw string. You can do that by placing the letter r before the string that you will print. Below is an example:

```
>>> print ( r"C:\Windows\notepad.exe" )

C:\Windows\notepad.exe

>>> _
```

Basic String Operations

In Python, you can perform operations on your strings. These basic string operations also use the common arithmetical operators, but when those operators are used on strings, they will produce different results. There are two of these. And they use the + and * operators. Below are examples on how to use them:

```
>>> print ( "cat" + "dog" )

catdog

>>> print ( "cat" * 3 )

catcatcat

>>> _
```

When the + operator is used between two strings, it will combine them. On the other hand, if the multiplication operator is used, the string will be repeated depending on the number indicated.

By the way, you cannot use operators between strings and numbers – with the exception of the multiplication symbol. For example:

```
>>> variable_x = 1 + "text"
```

The example above will return an unsupported operand type since Python does not know what to do when you add a string and a number.

Chapter 5: Transition from Interactive Mode to Programming Mode

Alright, by this time, you must already have a good feel on Python's interactive mode. You also know the basic concepts of variables, strings, and numbers. Now, it is time to put them together and create a simple program.

You can now close Python's window and open Notepad++. A new file should be currently opened once you open that program. The next step is to set the Language setting into Python. And save the file. Any name will do as long that you make sure that your file's extension is set to .py or Python file. In case the save function does not work, type anything on the text file. After you save it, remove the text you typed.

Now, you will start getting used to programming mode. Programming mode is where program development start. Unlike interactive mode, programming mode requires you to code first, save your file, and run it on Python. To get a feel of the programming mode, copy this sample below:

print ("Hello World!")

print ("This is a simple program that aims to display text.")

print ("That is all.")

input ("Press Enter Key to End this Program")

If you followed the instructions on the Getting Prepared chapter, press the F9 key. Once you do, Python will run and execute your script. It will be read line by line by Python just like in Interactive mode. The only difference is that the primary prompt is not there, and you cannot input any command while it is running.

Input Function

On the other hand, the example code uses the input function. The input function's purpose is to retrieve any text that the user will type in the program and wait for the Enter key to be pressed before going to the next line of code below it. And when the user presses the key the program will close since there are no remaining lines of code to execute.

By the way, if you remove the input function from the example, the program will just print the messages in it and close itself. And since Python will process those lines within split seconds, you will be unable to see if it work. So, in the following examples and lessons, the input function will be used to temporarily pause your scripts or prevent your program to close prematurely.

You can use the input function to assign values to variables. Check this example out:

print ("Can you tell me your name?")

name = input("Please type your name: ")

print ("Your name is " + name + ".")

print ("That is all.")

input ("Press Enter Key to End this Program. \n")

In this example, the variable name was assigned a value that will come from user input through the input function. When you run it, the program will pause on the Please type your name part and wait for user input. The user can place almost anything on it. And when he presses enter, Python will capture the text, and store it to variable name.

Once the name is established, the print function will confirm it and mention the content of the name variable.

Data Type Conversion

You can also use the input function to get numbers. However, to make sure the program will understand that its numbers that it will receive, make sure that your input does not include non-numeric characters. Below is a sample code of an adding program:

```
print ( "This program will add two numbers you would input." )

first_number = input ( "Type the first number: " )

second_number = input ( "Type the second number: " )

sum = int(first_number) + int(second_number)

print ( "The sum is " + str(sum) )

input ( "Press Enter Key to End this Program. \n" )
```

In this example, the program tries to get numbers from the user. And get the sum of those two numbers. However, there is a problem. The input function only produces string data. That means that even if you type in a number, the input will still assign a string version of that number to the variable.

And since they are both strings, you cannot add them as numbers. And if you do add them, it will result into a joined string. For example, if the first number was 1 and the second number was 2, the sum that will appear will be 12, which is mathematically wrong.

In order to fix that, you will need to convert the strings into its numeric form. In this example, they will be converted to integers. With the help of the int function, that can be easily done. Any variable will be converted to integer when placed inside the int function.

So, to get the integer sum of the first_number and second_number, both of them were converted into integers. By the way, converting only one of them will result into an error. With that done, the sum of the two numbers will be correctly produced, which 3.

Now the second roadblock is the print function. In the last print function, the example used an addition operator to join the The sum is text and the variable sum. However, since the variable sum is an integer, the operation will return an error. Just like before, you should convert the variable in order for the operation to work. In this case, the sum variable was converted to a string using the str function.

There are other data types in Python – just like with other programming languages. This part will not cover the technicalities of those data types and about the memory allocation given to them, but this part is to just familiarize you with it. Nevertheless, below is a list of a few of the data type conversion functions you might use while programming in Python:

- Long() – converts data to a long integer

- Hex() – converts integers to hexadecimal

- Float() – converts data to floating-point

- Unichr() – converts integers to Unicode

- Chr() – converts integers to characters

- Oct() – converts integers to octal

Chapter 6: Programming Mode – Conditional Statements

Just displaying text and getting text from user are not enough for you to make a decent program out of Python. You need your program to be capable of interacting with your user and be capable of producing results according to their inputs.

Because of that, you will need to use conditional statements. Conditional statements allow your program to execute code blocks according to the conditions you set. For you to get more familiar with conditional statements, check the example below:

```
print ( "Welcome to Guess the Number Game! " )

magic_number = input ( "Type your guess: " )

if ( magic_number == "1" ):

    print ( "You Win!" )

else:

    print ( "You Lose!" )

input ( "Press enter to exit this program " )
```

In this example, the if or conditional statement is used. The syntax of this function differs a bit from the other functions discussed earlier. In this one, you will need to set a conditional argument on its parentheses. The condition is that if the variable magic_number is equal to 1, then the code block under it will run. The colon after the condition indicates that it will have a code block beneath it.

When you go insert a code block under a statement, you will need to indent them. The code block under the if statement is print ("You Win!"). Because of that, it is and should be indented. If the condition is satisfied, which will happen if the user entered 1, then the code block under if will run. If the condition was not satisfied, it will be ignored, and Python will parse on the next line with the same indent level as if.

That next line will be the else statement. If and else go hand in hand. The have identical function. If their conditions are satisfied, then the program will run the code block underneath them. However, unlike if, else has a preset condition. Its condition is that whenever the previous conditional statement is not satisfied, then it will run its code block. And that also means that if the previous conditional statement's condition was satisfied, it will not run.

Due to that, if the user guesses the right magic number, then the code block of if will run and the else statement's code block will be ignored. If the user was unable to guess the right magic number, if's code block will be ignored and else's code block will run.

Conclusion

Thank you again for purchasing this book!

I hope this book was able to help you to understand the basic concepts of programming and become familiar in Python in just one day.

The next step is to research and learn looping in Python. Loops are control structures that can allow your program to repeat various code blocks. They are very similar to conditional statements. The only difference is that, their primary function is to repeat all the lines of codes placed inside their codeblocks. Also, whenever the parser of Python reaches the end of its code block, it will go back to the loop statement and see if the condition is still satisfied. In case that it is, it will loop again. In case that it does not, it will skip its code block and move to the next line with the same indent level.

In programming, loops are essential. Truth be told, loops compose most functionalities of complex programs. Also, when it comes to coding efficiency, loops makes program shorter and faster to develop. Using loops in your programs will reduce the size of your codes. And it will reduce the amount of time you need to write all the codes you need to achieve the function you desire in your program.

If you do not use loops in your programs, you will need to repeat typing or pasting lines of codes that might span to hundreds of instances – whereas if you use loops in your programs, those hundred instances can be reduced into five or seven lines of codes.

There are multiple methods on how you can create a loop in your program. Each loop method or function has their unique purposes. Trying to imitate another loop method with one loop method can be painstaking.

On the other hand, once you are done with loops, you will need to upgrade your current basic knowledge about Python. Research about all the other operators that were not mentioned in this book, the other data types and their quirks and functions, simple statements, compound statements, and top-level components.

Programming Box Set #30: Python Programming in a Day & C Programming Success in a Day & C Programming Professional Made Easy

To be honest, Python is huge. You have just seen a small part of it. And once you delve deeper on its other capabilities and the possible things you could create with it, you will surely get addicted to programming.

Finally, if you enjoyed this book, please take the time to share your thoughts and post a review on Amazon. We do our best to reach out to readers and provide the best value we can. Your positive review will help us achieve that. It'd be greatly appreciated!

Thank you and good luck!

Book 2

C Programming Success in a Day

BY SAM KEY

Beginners' Guide To Fast, Easy And Efficient Learning Of C Programming

Programming Box Set #30: Python Programming in a Day & C Programming Success in a Day & C Programming Professional Made Easy

Copyright 2015 by Sam Key - All rights reserved.

Table Contents

Introduction

I want to thank you and congratulate you for purchasing the book, "C Programming Success in a Day – Beginners guide to fast, easy and efficient learning of Cc programming".

C. is one of the most popular and most used programming languages back then and today. Many expert developers have started with learning C in order to become knowledgeable in computer programming. In some grade schools and high schools, C programming is included on their curriculum.

If you are having doubts learning the language, do not. C is actually easy to learn. Compared to C++, C is much simpler and offer little. You do not need spend years to become a master of this language.

This book will tackle the basics when it comes to C. It will cover the basic functions you need in order to create programs that can produce output and accept input. Also, in the later chapters, you will learn how to make your program capable of simple thinking. And lastly, the last chapters will deal with teaching you how to create efficient programs with the help of loops.

Anyway, before you start programming using C, you need to get some things ready. First, you will need a compiler. A compiler is a program that will translate, compile, or convert your lines of code as an executable file. It means that, you will need a compiler for you to be able to run the program you have developed.

In case you are using this book as a supplementary source of information and you are taking a course of C, you might already have a compiler given to you by your instructor. If you are not, you can get one of the compilers that are available on the internet from MinGW.org.

You will also need a text editor. One of the best text editors you can use is Notepad++. It is free and can be downloadable from the internet. Also, it works well with MinGW's compiler.

In case you do not have time to configure or install those programs, you can go and get Microsoft's Visual C++ program. It contains all the things you need in order to practice developing programs using C or C++.

The content of this book was simplified in order for you to comprehend the ideas and practices in developing programs in C easily. Thanks again for purchasing this book. I hope you enjoy it!

Chapter 1: Hello World – the Basics

When coding a C program, you must start your code with the function 'main'. By the way, a function is a collection of action that aims to achieve one or more goals. For example, a vegetable peeler has one function, which is to remove a skin of a vegetable. The peeler is composed of parts (such as the blade and handle) that will aid you to perform its function. A C function is also composed of such components and they are the lines of codes within it.

Also, take note that in order to make your coding life easier, you will need to include some prebuilt headers or functions from your compiler.

To give you an idea on what C code looks like, check the sample below:

```c
#include <stdio.h>

int main()

{

        printf( "Hello World!\n" );

        getchar();

        return 0;

}
```

As you can see in the first line, the code used the #include directive to include the stdio.h in the program. In this case, the stdio.h will provide you with access to functions such as printf and getchar.

Main Declaration

After that, the second line contains int main(). This line tells the compiler that there exist a function named main. The int in the line indicates that the function main will return an integer or number.

Curly Braces

The next line contains a curly brace. In C programming, curly braces indicate the start and end of a code block or a function. A code block is a series of codes joined together in a series. When a function is called by the program, all the line of codes inside it will be executed.

Printf()

The printf function, which follows the opening curly brace is the first line of code in your main function or code block. Like the function main, the printf also have a code block within it, which is already created and included since you included <stdio.h> in your program. The function of printf is to print text into your program's display window.

Beside printf is the value or text that you want to print. It should be enclosed in parentheses to abide standard practice. The value that the code want to print is Hello World!. To make sure that printf to recognize that you want to print a string and display the text properly, it should be enclosed inside double quotation marks.

By the way, in programming, a single character is called a character while a sequence of characters is called a string.

Escape Sequence

You might have noticed that the sentence is followed by a \n. In C, \n means new line. Since your program will have problems if you put a new line or press enter on the value of the printf, it is best to use its text equivalent or the escape sequence of the new line.

By the way, the most common escape sequences used in C are:

\t = tab

\f = new page

\r = carriage return

\b = backspace

\v = vertical tab

Semicolons

After the last parenthesis, a semicolon follows. And if you look closer, almost every line of code ends with it. The reasoning behind that is that the semicolon acts as an indicator that it is the end of the line of code or command. Without it, the compiler will think that the following lines are included in the printf function. And if that happens, you will get a syntax error.

Getchar()

Next is the getchar() function. Its purpose is to receive user input from the keyboard. Many programmers use it as a method on pausing a program and letting the program wait for the user to interact with it before it executes the next line of code. To make the program move through after the getchar() function, the user must press the enter key.

In the example, if you compile or run it without getchar(), the program will open the display or the console, display the text, and then immediately close. Without the break provided by the getchar() function, the computer will execute those commands instantaneously. And the program will open and close so fast that you will not be able to even see the Hello World text in the display.

Return Statement

The last line of code in the function is return 0. The return statement is essential in function blocks. When the program reaches this part, the return statement will tell the program its value. Returning the 0 value will make the program interpret that the function or code block that was executed successfully.

And at the last line of the example is the closing curly brace. It signifies that the program has reached the end of the function.

It was not that not hard, was it? With that example alone, you can create simple programs that can display text. Play around with it a bit and familiarize yourself with C's basic syntax.

Chapter 2: Basic Input Output

After experimenting with what you learned in the previous chapter, you might have realized that it was not enough. It was boring. And just displaying what you typed in your program is a bit useless.

This time, this chapter will teach you how to create a program that can interact with the user. Check this code example:

```
#include <stdio.h>

int main()

{

        int number_container;

        printf( "Enter any number you want! " );

        scanf( "%d", &number_container );

        printf( "The number you entered is %d", number_container );

        getchar();

        return 0;

}
```

Variables

You might have noticed the int number_container part in the first line of the code block. int number_container is an example of variable declaration. To declare a variable in C, you must indicate the variable type first, and then the name of the variable name.

In the example, int was indicated as the variable or data type, which means the variable is an integer. There are other variable types in C such as float for floating-point numbers, char for characters, etc. Alternatively, the name number_container was indicated as the variable's name or identifier.

Variables are used to hold values throughout the program and code blocks. The programmer can let them assign a value to it and retrieve its value when it is needed.

For example:

int number_container;

number_container = 3;

printf ("The variables value is %d", number_container);

In that example, the first line declared that the program should create an integer variable named number_container. The second line assigned a value to the variable. And the third line makes the program print the text together with the value of the variable. When executed, the program will display:

The variables value is 3

You might have noticed the %d on the printf line on the example. The %d part indicates that the next value that will be printed will be an integer. Also, the quotation on the printf ended after %d. Why is that?

In order to print the value of a variable, it must be indicated with the double quotes. If you place double quotes on the variables name, the compiler will treat it as a literal string. If you do this:

int number_container;

number_container = 3;

printf ("The variables value is number_container");

The program will display:

The variables value is number_container

By the way, you can also use %i as a replacement for %d.

Assigning a value to a variable is simple. Just like in the previous example, just indicate the name of variable, follow it with an equal sign, and declare its value.

When creating variables, you must make sure that each variable will have unique names. Also, the variables should never have the same name as functions. In addition, you can declare multiple variables in one line by using commas. Below is an example:

int first_variable, second_variable, third_variable;

Those three variables will be int type variables. And again, never forget to place a semicolon after your declaration.

When assigning a value or retrieving the value of a variable, make sure that you declare its existence first. If not, the compiler will return an error since it will try to access something that does not exist yet.

Scanf()

In the first example in this chapter, you might have noticed the scanf function. The scanf function is also included in the <stdio.h>. Its purpose is to retrieve text user input from the user.

After the program displays the 'Enter any number you want' text, it will proceed in retrieving a number from the user. The cursor will be appear after the text since the new line escape character was no included in the printf.

The cursor will just blink and wait for the user to enter any characters or numbers. To let the program get the number the user typed and let it proceed to the next line of code, he must press the Enter key. Once he does that, the program will display the text 'The number you entered is' and the value of the number the user inputted a while ago.

To make the scanf function work, you must indicate the data type it needs to receive and the location of the variable where the value that scanf will get will be stored. In the example:

scanf("%d", &number_container);

The first part "%d" indicates that the scanf function must retrieve an integer. On the other hand, the next part indicates the location of the variable. You must have noticed the ampersand placed in front of the variable's name. The ampersand retrieves the location of the variable and tells it to the function.

Unlike the typical variable value assignment, scanf needs the location of the variable instead of its name alone. Due to that, without the ampersand, the function will not work.

Math or Arithmetic Operators

Aside from simply giving number variables with values by typing a number, you can assign values by using math operators. In C, you can add, subtract, multiply, and divide numbers and assign the result to variables directly. For example:

int sum;

sum = 1 + 2;

If you print the value of sum, it will return a 3, which is the result of the addition of 1 and 2. By the way, the + sign is for addition, - for subtraction, * for multiplication, and / for division.

With the things you have learned as of now, you can create a simple calculator program. Below is an example code:

```c
#include <stdio.h>

int main()
{
        int first_addend, second_addend, sum;
        printf( "Enter the first addend! " );
        scanf( "%d", &first_addend );
        printf( "\nEnter the second addend! " );
        scanf( "%d", &second_addend );
        sum = first_addend + second_addend;
        printf( "The sum of the two numbers is %d", sum );
        getchar();
        return 0;
}
```

Chapter 3: Conditional Statements

The calculator program seems nice, is it not? However, the previous example limits you on creating programs that only uses one operation, which is a bit disappointing. Well, in this chapter, you can improve that program with the help of if or conditional statements. And of course, learning this will improve your overall programming skills. This is the part where you will be able to make your program 'think'.

'If' statements can allow you to create branches in your code blocks. Using them allows you to let the program think and perform specific functions or actions depending on certain variables and situations. Below is an example:

```c
#include <stdio.h>

int main()

{

        int some_number;

        printf( "Welcome to Guess the Magic Number program. \n" );

        printf( "Guess the magic number to win. \n" );

        printf( "Type the magic number and press Enter: " );

        scanf( "%d", &some_number );

        if ( some_number == 3 ) {

                printf( "You guessed the right number! " );

        }

        getchar();

        return 0;

}
```

In the example, the if statement checked if the value of the variable some_number is equal to number 3. In case the user entered the number 3 on the program, the comparison between the variable some_number and three will return TRUE since the value of some_number 3 is true. Since the value that the if statement received was TRUE, then it will process the code block below it. And the result will be:

You guessed the right number!

If the user input a number other than three, the comparison will return a FALSE value. If that happens, the program will skip the code block in the if statement and proceed to the next line of code after the if statement's code block.

By the way, remember that you need to use the curly braces to enclosed the functions that you want to happen in case your if statement returns TRUE. Also, when inserting if statement, you do not need to place a semicolon after the if statement or its code block's closing curly brace. However, you will still need to place semicolons on the functions inside the code blocks of your if statements.

TRUE and FALSE

The if statement will always return TRUE if the condition is satisfied. For example, the condition in the if statement is 10 > 2. Since 10 is greater than 2, then it is true. On the other hand, the if statement will always return FALSE if the condition is not satisfied. For example, the condition in the if statement is 5 < 5. Since 5 is not less than 5, then the statement will return a FALSE.

Note that if statements only return two results: TRUE and FALSE. In computer programming, the number equivalent to TRUE is any nonzero number. In some cases, it is only the number 1. On the other hand, the number equivalent of FALSE is zero.

Operators

Also, if statements use comparison, Boolean, or relational and logical operators. Some of those operators are:

== – equal to

!= – not equal to

> – greater than

< – less than

>= – greater than or equal to

<= – less than or equal to

Else Statement

There will be times that you would want your program to do something else in case your if statement return FALSE. And that is what the else statement is for. Check the example below:

```
#include <stdio.h>

int main()

{

        int some_number;

        printf( "Welcome to Guess the Magic Number program. \n" );

        printf( "Guess the magic number to win. \n" );

        printf( "Type the magic number and press Enter: " );

        scanf( "%d", &some_number );

        if ( some_number == 3 ) {

                printf( "You guessed the right number! " );
```

```
}

else {

        printf( "Sorry. That is the wrong number" );

}

getchar();

return 0;

}
```

If ever the if statement returns FALSE, the program will skip next to the else statement immediately. And since the if statement returns FALSE, it will immediately process the code block inside the else statement.

For example, if the number the user inputted on the program is 2, the if statement will return a FALSE. Due to that, the else statement will be processed, and the program will display:

Sorry. That is the wrong number

On the other hand, if the if statement returns TRUE, it will process the if statement's code block, but it will bypass all the succeeding else statements below it.

Else If

If you want more conditional checks on your program, you will need to take advantage of else if. Else if is a combination of the if and else statement. It will act like an else statement, but instead of letting the program execute the code block below it, it will perform another check as if it was an if statement. Below is an example:

```c
#include <stdio.h>

int main()

{

        int some_number;

        printf( "Welcome to Guess the Magic Number program. \n" );

        printf( "Guess the magic number to win. \n" );

        printf( "Type the magic number and press Enter: " );

        scanf( "%d", &some_number );

        if ( some_number == 3 ) {

                printf( "You guessed the right number! " );

        }

        else if ( some_number > 3 ){

                printf( "Your guess is too high!" );

        }

        else {

                printf( "Your guess is too low!" );

        }

        getchar();

        return 0;

}
```

In case the if statement returns FALSE, the program will evaluate the else if statement. If it returns TRUE, it will execute its code block and ignore the following else statements. However, if it is FALSE, it will proceed on the last else statement, and execute its code block. And just like before, if the first if statement returns true, it will disregard the following else and else if statements.

In the example, if the user inputs 3, he will get the You guessed the right number message. If the user inputs 4 or higher, he will get the Your guess is too high message. And if he inputs any other number, he will get a Your guess is too low message since any number aside from 3 and 4 or higher is automatically lower than 3.

With the knowledge you have now, you can upgrade the example calculator program to handle different operations. Look at the example and study it:

```c
#include <stdio.h>

int main()

{

        int first_number, second_number, result, operation;

        printf( "Enter the first number: " );

        scanf( "%d", &first_number );

        printf( "\nEnter the second number: " );

        scanf( "%d", &second_number );

        printf ( "What operation would you like to use? \n" );

        printf ( "Enter 1 for addition. \n" );

        printf ( "Enter 2 for subtraction. \n" );

        printf ( "Enter 3 for multiplication. \n" );

        printf ( "Enter 4 for division. \n" );
```

```c
scanf( "%d", &operation );

if ( operation == 1 ) {

        result = first_number + second_number;

        printf( "The sum is %d", result );

}

else if ( operation == 2 ){

        result = first_number - second_number;

        printf( "The difference is %d", result );

}

else if ( operation == 3 ){

        result = first_number * second_number;

        printf( "The product is %d", result );

}

else if ( operation == 4 ){

        result = first_number / second_number;

        printf( "The quotient is %d", result );

}

else {

        printf( "You have entered an invalid choice." );

}

getchar();

return 0;

}
```

Chapter 4: Looping in C

The calculator's code is getting better, right? As of now, it is possible that you are thinking about the programs that you could create with the usage of the conditional statements.

However, as you might have noticed in the calculator program, it seems kind of painstaking to use. You get to only choose one operation every time you run the program. When the calculation ends, the program closes. And that can be very annoying and unproductive.

To solve that, you must create loops in the program. Loops are designed to let the program execute some of the functions inside its code blocks. It effectively eliminates the need to write some same line of codes. It saves the time of the programmer and it makes the program run more efficiently.

There are four different ways in creating a loop in C. In this chapter, two of the only used and simplest loop method will be discussed. To grasp the concept of looping faster, check the example below:

```
#include <stdio.h>

int main()

{

        int some_number;

        int guess_result;

        guess_result = 0;


        printf( "Welcome to Guess the Magic Number program. \n" );

        printf( "Guess the magic number to win. \n" );

        printf( "You have unlimited chances to guess the number. \n" );
```

```c
while ( guess_result == 0 ) {


        printf( "Guess the magic number: " );

        scanf( "%d", &some_number );

        if ( some_number == 3 ) {

                printf( "You guessed the right number! \n" );

                guess_result = 1;

        }

        else if ( some_number > 3 ){

                printf( "Your guess is too high! \n" );

                guess_result = 0;

        }

        else {

                printf( "Your guess is too low! \n" );

                guess_result = 0;

        }

}

printf( "Thank you for playing. Press Enter to exit this program." );

getchar();

return 0;

}
```

While Loop

In this example, the while loop function was used. The while loop allows the program to execute the code block inside it as long as the condition is met or the argument in it returns TRUE. It is one of the simplest loop function in C. In the example, the condition that the while loop requires is that the guess_result variable should be equal to 0.

As you can see, in order to make sure that the while loop will start, the value of the guess_result variable was set to 0.

If you have not noticed it yet, you can actually nest code blocks within code blocks. In this case, the code block of the if and else statements were inside the code block of the while statement.

Anyway, every time the code reaches the end of the while statement and the guess_result variable is set to 0, it will repeat itself. And to make sure that the program or user experience getting stuck into an infinite loop, a safety measure was included.

In the example, the only way to escape the loop is to guess the magic number. If the if statement within the while code block was satisfied, its code block will run. In that code block, a line of code sets the variable guess_result's value to 1. This effectively prevent the while loop from running once more since the guess_result's value is not 0 anymore, which makes the statement return a FALSE.

Once that happens, the code block of the while loop and the code blocks inside it will be ignored. It will skip to the last printf line, which will display the end program message 'Thank you for playing. Press Enter to exit this program'.

For Loop

The for loop is one of the most handy looping function in C. And its main use is to perform repetitive commands on a set number of times. Below is an example of its use:

```c
#include <stdio.h>

int main()

{

        int some_number;

        int x;

        int y;


        printf( "Welcome to Guess the Magic Number program. \n" );

        printf( "Guess the magic number to win. \n" );

        printf( "You have only three chance of guessing. \n" );

        printf( "If you do not get the correct answer after guessing three times. \n"
        );

        printf( "This program will be terminated. \n" );


        for (x = 0; x < 3; x++) {

                y = 3 - x;

                printf( "The number of guesses that you have left is: %d", y );

                printf( "\nGuess the magic number: " );

                scanf( "%d", &some_number );

                if ( some_number == 3 ) {

                        printf( "You guessed the right number! \n" );

                        x = 4;

                }

                else if ( some_number > 3 ){
```

```
                printf( "Your guess is too high! \n " );

        }

        else {

                printf( "Your guess is too low! \n " );

        }

    }

    printf( "Press the Enter button to close this program. \n" );

    getchar();

    getchar();

    return 0;

}
```

The for statement's argument section or part requires three things. First, the initial value of the variable that will be used. In this case, the example declared that x = 0. Second, the condition. In the example, the for loop will run until x has a value lower than 3. Third, the variable update line. Every time the for loop loops, the variable update will be executed. In this case, the variable update that will be triggered is x++.

Increment and Decrement Operators

By the way, x++ is a variable assignment line. The x is the variable and the ++ is an increment operator. The function of an increment operator is to add 1 to the variable where it was placed. In this case, every time the program reads x++, the program will add 1 to the variable x. If x has a value of 10, the increment operator will change variable x's value to 11.

On the other hand, you can also use the decrement operator instead of the increment operator. The decrement operator is done by place -- next to a variable. Unlike the increment operator, the decrement subtracts 1 to its operand.

Just like the while loop, the for loop will run as long as its condition returns TRUE. However, the for loop has a built in safety measure and variable declaration. You do not need to declare the value needed for its condition outside the statement. And the safety measure to prevent infinite loop is the variable update. However, it does not mean that it will be automatically immune to infinite loops. Poor programming can lead to it. For example:

```
for (x = 1; x > 1; x++) {

        /* Insert Code Block Here */

}
```

In this example, the for loop will enter into an infinite loop unless a proper means of escape from the loop is coded inside its code block.

The structure of the for loop example is almost the same with while loop. The only difference is that the program is set to loop for only three times. In this case, it only allows the user to guess three times or until the value of variable x does not reach 3 or higher.

Every time the user guesses wrong, the value of x is incremented, which puts the loop closer in ending. However, in case the user guesses right, the code block of the if statement assigns a value higher than 3 to variable x in order to escape the loop and end the program.

Conclusion

Thank you again for purchasing this book!

I hope this book was able to help you to learn the basics of C programming. The next step is to learn the other looping methods, pointers, arrays, strings, command line arguments, recursion, and binary trees.

Finally, if you enjoyed this book, please take the time to share your thoughts and post a review on Amazon. We do our best to reach out to readers and provide the best value we can. Your positive review will help us achieve that. It'd be greatly appreciated!

Thank you and good luck!

Book 3
C Programming Professional
Made Easy

Sam Key

Expert C Programming Language Success In A Day For Any Computer User!

Programming Box Set #30: Python Programming in a Day & C Programming Success in a Day & C Programming Professional Made Easy

Table Of Contents

Introduction

I want to thank you and congratulate you for purchasing the book, "Professional C Programming Made Easy: Expert C Programming Language Success In A Day For Any Computer User!".

This book contains proven steps and strategies on how to understand and perform C programming. C is one of the most basic programming tools used for a wide array of applications. Most people stay away from it because the language seem complicated, with all those characters, letters, sequences and special symbols.

This book will break down every element and explain in detail each language used in the C program. By the time you are done with this book, C programming language will be easy to understand and easy to execute.

Read on and learn.

Thanks again for purchasing this book. I hope you enjoy it!

Chapter 1 The Basic Elements Of C

The seemingly complicated C program is composed of the following basic elements:

Character Set

The alphabet in both upper and lower cases is used in C. The 0-9 digits are also used, including white spaces and some special characters. These are used in different combinations to form elements of a basic C program such as expressions, constants, variables, etc.

Special characters include the following:

+ ,. *− / % = & ! #?"^ '| / ( )< > { } [ ] ;: @ ~!

White spaces include:

- Blank space

- Carriage return

- Horizontal tab

- Form feed

- New line

Identifiers

An identifier is a name given to the various elements of the C program, such as arrays, variables and functions. These contain digits and letters in various arrangements. However, identifiers should always start with a letter. The letters may be in upper case, lower case or both. However, these are not interchangeable. C programming is case sensitive, as each letter in different cases is regarded as separate from each other. Underscores are also permitted because it is considered by the program as a kind of letter.

Examples of valid identifiers include the following:

ab123

A

stud_name

average

velocity

TOTAL

Identifiers need to start with a letter and should not contain illegal characters. Examples of invalid identifiers include the following:

2nd	- should always start with a letter
"Jamshedpur"	- contains the illegal character (")
stud name	- contains a blank space, which is an illegal character
stud-name	- contains an illegal character (-)

In C, a single identifier may be used to refer to a number of different entities within the same C program. For instance, an array and a variable can share one identifier. For example:

The variable is int difference, average, A[5]; // sum, average

The identifier is A[5].

In the same program, an array can be named A, too.

__func__

The __func__ is a predefined identifier that provides functions names and makes these accessible and ready for use anytime in the function. The complier would automatically declare the __func__ immediately after placing the opening brace when declaring the function definitions. The compiler declares the predefined identifier this way:

static const char __func__[] = "Alex";

"Alex" refers to a specific name of this particular function.

Take a look at this example:

```
#include <stdio.h>


void anna1(void)  {
    printf("%sn",__func__);
    return;
}
```

```
int main() {

    myfunc();

}
```

What will appear as an output will be anna1

Keywords

Reserved words in C that come with standard and predefined meanings are called keywords. The uses for these words are restricted to their predefined intended purpose. Keywords cannot be utilized as programmer-defined identifiers. In C, there are 32 keywords being used, which include the following:

auto	return
break	sizeof
char	signed
case	switch
continue	typedef
const	struct
do	union
default	switch
double	void
float	unsigned
else	while
extern	volatile
enum	
goto	
for	
if	
long	
int	
register	
short	

Data Types

There are different types of data values that are passed in C. Each of the types of data has different representations within the memory bank of the computer. These also have varying memory requirements. Data type modifiers/qualifiers are often used to augment the different types of data.

Supported data types in C include int, char, float, double, void, _Bool, _Complex, arrays, and constants.

int

Integer quantities are stored in this type of data. The data type *int* can store a collection of different values, starting from INT_MAX to INT_MIN. An in-header file, <limits h>, defines the range.

These int data types use type modifiers such as unsigned, signed, long, long long and short.

Short int means that they occupy memory space of only 2 bytes.

A long int uses 4 bytes of memory space.

Short unsigned int is a data type that uses 2 bytes of memory space and store positive values only, ranging from 0 to 65535.

Unsigned int requires memory space similar to that of short unsigned int. For regular and ordinary int, the bit at the leftmost portion is used for the integer's sign.

Long unsigned int uses 4 bytes of space. It stores all positive integers ranging from 0 to 4294967295.

An int data is automatically considered as signed.

Long long int data type uses 64 bits memory. This type may either be unsigned or signed. Signed long long data type can store values ranging from −9,223,372,036,854,775,808 to 9,223,372,036,854,775,807. Unsigned long long data type stores value range of 0 to 18,446,744,073,709,551,615.

char

Single characters such as those found in C program's character set are stored by this type of data. The char data type uses 1 byte in the computer's memory. Any value from C program's character set can be stored as char. Modifiers that can be used are either unsigned or signed.

A char would always use 1 byte in the computer's memory space, whether it is signed or unsigned. The difference is on the value range. Values that can be stored as unsigned char range from 0 to 255. Signed char stores values ranging from −128 to +127. By default, a char data type is considered unsigned.

For each of the char types, there is a corresponding integer interpretation. This makes each char a special short integer.

float

A float is a data type used in storing real numbers that have single precision. That is, precision denoted as having 6 more digits after a decimal point. Float data type uses 4 bytes memory space.

The modifier for this data type is long, which uses the same memory space as that of double data type.

double

The double data type is used for storing real numbers that have double precision. Memory space used is 8 bytes. Double data type uses long as a type modifier. This uses up memory storage space of 10 bytes.

void

Void data type is used for specifying empty sets, which do not contain any value. Hence, void data type also occupies no space (0 bytes) in the memory storage.

_Bool

This is a Boolean type of data. It is an unsigned type of integer. It stores only 2 values, which is 0 and 1. When using _Bool, include **<stdboolh>**.

_Complex

This is used for storing complex numbers. In C, three types of _Complex are used. There is the float _Complex, double _Complex, and long double _Complex. These are found in <complex h> file.

Arrays

This identifier is used in referring to the collection of data that share the same name and of the same type of data. For example, all integers or all characters that have the same name. Each of the data is represented by its own array element. The subscripts differentiate the arrays from each other.

Constants

Constants are identifiers used in C. The values of identifiers do not change anywhere within the program. Constants are declared this way:

const datatype varname = value

const is the keyword that denotes or declares the variable as the fixed value entity, i.e., the constant.

In C, there are 4 basic constants used. These include the integer constant, floating-point, character and string constants. Floating-point and integer types of constant do not contain any blank spaces or commas. Minus signs can be used, which denotes negative quantities.

Integer Constants

Integer constants are integer valued numbers consisting of sequence of digits. These can be written using 3 different number systems, namely, decimal, octal and hexadecimal.

Decimal system (base 10)

An integer constant written in the decimal system contains combinations of numbers ranging from 0 to 9. Decimal constants should start with any number other except 0. For example, a decimal constant is written in C as:

const int size =76

Octal (base 8)

Octal constants are any number combinations from 0 to 7. To identify octal constants, the first number should be 0. For example:

const int a= 043; const int b=0;

An octal constant is denoted in the binary form. Take the octal 0347. Each digit is represented as:

$0347 = 011\ 100\ 111 = 3 * 8^2 + 4 * 8^1 + 7 * 8^0 = 231$

3 4 7

Hexadecimal constant (base 16)

This type consists of any of the possible combinations of digits ranging from 0 to 9. This type also includes letters a to f, written in either lowercase or uppercase. To identify hexadecimal constants, these should start with 0X or 0X. For example:

const int c= 0x7FF;

For example, the hexadecimal number 0x2A5 is internally represented in bit patterns within C as:

$0x2A5 = 0010\ 1010\ 0101 = 2 * 16^2 + 10 * 16^1 + 5 * 16^0 = 677$

2   A   5

Wherein, 677 is the decimal equivalent of the hexadecimal number 0x2.

Prefixes for integer constants can either be long or unsigned. A long integer constant (long int) ends with a l of L, such as 67354L or 67354l. The last portion of an unsigned long integer constant should either be ul or UL, such as 672893UL or 672893ul. For an unsigned long long integer constant, UL or ul should be at the last portion. An unsigned constant should end with U or u, such as 673400095u or 673400095U. Normal integer constants are written without any suffix, such as a simple 67458.

Floating Point Constant

This type of constant has a base 10 or base 16 and contains an exponent, a decimal point or both. For a floating point constant with a base 10 and a decimal point, the base is replaced by an E or e. For example, the constant $1.8 *10^-3$ is written as 1.8e-3 or 1.8E-3.

For hexadecimal character constants and the exponent is in the binary form, the exponent is replaced by P or p. Take a look at this example:

This type of constant is often precision quantities. These occupy around 8 bytes of memory. Different add-ons are allowed in some C program versions, such as F for a single precision floating constant or L for a long floating point type of constant.

Character Constant

A sequence of characters, whether single or multiple ones, enclosed by apostrophes or single quotation marks is called a character constant. The character set in the computer determines the integer value equivalent to each character constant. Escape sequences may also be found within the sequence of a character constant.

Single character constants enclosed by apostrophes is internally considered as integers. For example, 'A' is a single character constant that has an integer value of 65. The corresponding integer value is also called the ASCII value. Because of the corresponding numerical value, single character constants can be used in calculations just like how integers are used. Also, these constants can also be used when comparing other types of character constants.

Prefixes used in character constants such as L, U or u are used for character literals. These are considered as wide types of character constants. Character literals with the prefix L are considered under the type wchar_t, which are defined as <stddef.h> under the header file. Character constants that use the prefix U or u are considered as type char16_t or char32_t. These are considered as unsigned types of characters and are defined under the header file as <uchar.h>.

Those that do not have the prefix L are considered a narrow or ordinary character constant. Those that have escape sequences or are composed of at least 2 characters are considered as multicharacter constants.

Escape sequences are a type of character constant used in expressing non-printing characters like carriage return or tab. This sequence always begins with a backward slash, followed by special characters. These sequences represent a single character in the C language even if they are composed of more than 1 character. Examples of some of the most common escape sequences, and their integer (ASCII) value, used in C include the following:

Character	Escape Sequence	ASCII Value
Backspace	\b	008
Bell	\a	007
Newline	\n	010
Null	\0	000
Carriage	\r	013
Horizontal tab	\t	009
Vertical tab	\v	011
Form feed	\f	012

String Literals

Multibyte characters that form a sequence are called string literals. Multibyte characters have bit representations that fit into 1 or more bytes. String literals are enclosed within double quotation marks, for example, "A" and "Anna". There are 2 types of string literals, namely, UTF-8 string literals and wide string literals. Prefixes used for wide string literals include u, U or L. Prefix for UTF-8 string literals is u8.

Additional characters or extended character sets included in string literals are recognized and supported by the compiler. These additional characters can be used meaningfully to further enhance character constants and string literals.

Symbolic constants

Symbolic constants are substitute names for numeric, string or character constants within a program. The compiler would replace the symbolic constants with its actual value once the program is run.

At the beginning of the program, the symbolic constant is defined with a **#define** feature. This feature is called the preprocessor directive.

The definition of a symbolic constant does not end with a semi colon, like other C statements. Take a look at this example:

#define PI 3.1415

(//PI is the constant that will represent value 3.1415)

#define True 1

#define name "Alice"

For all numeric constants such as floating point and integer, non-numeric characters and blank spaces are not included. These constants are also limited by minimum and maximum bounds, which are usually dependent on the computer.

Variables

Memory locations where data is stored are called variables. These are indicated by a unique identifier. Names for variables are symbolic representations that refer to a particular memory location. Examples are *count, car_no* and *sum*.

Rules when writing the variable names

Writing variable names follow certain rules in order to make sure that data is stored properly and retrieved efficiently.

- Letters (in both lowercase and uppercase), underscore ('_') and digits are the only characters that can be used for variable names.

- Variables should begin either with an underscore or a letter. Starting with an underscore is acceptable, but is not highly recommended. Underscores at the beginning of variables can come in conflict with system names and the compiler may protest.

- There is no limit on the length of variables. The compiler can distinguish the first 31 characters of a variable. This means that individual variables should have different sequences for the 1st 31 characters.

Variables should also be declared at the beginning of a program before it can be used.

Chapter 2 What is C Programming Language?

In C, the programming language is a language that focuses on the structure. It was developed in 1972, at Bell Laboratories, by Dennis Ritchie. The features of the language were derived from "B", which is an earlier programming language and formally known as BCPL or Basic Combined Programming Language. The C programming language was originally developed to implement the UNIX operating system.

Standards of C Programming Language

In 1989, the American National Standards Institute developed the 1st standard specifications. This pioneering standard specification was referred to as C89 and C90, both referring to the same programming language.

In 1999, a revision was made in the programming language. The revised standard was called C99. It had new features such as advanced data types. It also had a few changes, which gave rise to more applications.

The C11 standard was developed, which added new features to the programming language for C. This had a library-like generic macro type, enhanced Unicode support, anonymous structures, multi-threading, bounds-checked functions and atomic structures. It had improved compatibility with C++. Some parts of the C99 library in C11 were made optional.

The Embedded C programming language included a few features that were not part of C. These included the named address spaces, basic I/O hardware addressing and fixed point arithmetic.

C Programming Language Features

There are a lot of features of the programming language, which include the following:

- Modularity

- Interactivity

- Portability

- Reliability

- Effectiveness

- Efficiency

- Flexibility

Uses of the C Programming Language

This language has found several applications. It is now used for the development of system applications, which form a huge portion of operating systems such as Linux, Windows and UNIX.

Some of the applications of C language include the following:

- Spreadsheets

- Database systems

- Word processors

- Graphics packages

- Network drivers

- Compilers and Assemblers

- Operating system development

- Interpreters

Chapter 3 Understanding C Program

The C program has several features and steps in order for an output or function is carried out.

Basic Commands (for writing basic C Program)

The basic syntax and commands used in writing a simple C program include the following:

#include <stdio.h>

This command is a preprocessor. <stdio.h> stands for standard input output header file. This is a file from the C library, which is included before the C program is compiled.

int main()

Execution of all C program begins with this main function.

{

This symbol is used to indicate the start of the main function.

}

This indicates the conclusion of the main function.

/* */

Anything written in between this command will not be considered for execution and compilation.

printf (output);

The printf command prints the output on the screen.

getch();

Writing this command would allow the system to wait for any keyboard character input.

return 0

Writing this command will terminate the C program or main function and return to 0.

A basic C Program would look like this:

```c
#include <stdio.h>
int main()
{
/* Our first simple C basic program */
printf("Hello People! ");
getch();
return 0;
}
```

The output of this simple program would look like this:

Hello People!

Chapter 4 Learn C Programming

After learning the basic elements and what the language is all about, time to start programming in C. Here are the most important steps:

Download a compiler

A compiler is a program needed to compile the C code. It interprets the written codes and translates it into specific signals, which can be understood by the computer. Usually, compiler programs are free. There are different compilers available for several operating systems. Microsoft Visual Studio and MinGW are compilers available for Windows operating systems. XCode is among the best compilers for Mac. Among the most widely used C compiler options for Linux is gcc.

Basic Codes

Consider the following example of a simple C program in the previous chapter:

```
#include <stdio.h>


int main()

{

    printf("Hello People!\n");

    getchar();

    return 0;

}
```

At the start of the program, #include command is placed. This is important in order to load the libraries where the needed functions are located.

The <stdio.h> refers to the file library and allows for the use of the succeeding functions getchar() and printf().

The command int main () sends a message to the compiler to run the function with the name "main" and return a certain integer once it is done running. Every C program executes a main function.

The symbol { } is used to specify that everything within it is a component of the "main" function that the compiler should run.

The function printf() tells the system to display the words or characters within the parenthesis onto the computer screen. The quotation marks make certain that the C compiler would print the words or characters as it is. The sequence \n informs the C compiler to place its cursor to the succeeding line. At the conclusion of the line, a ; (semicolon) is placed to denote that the sequence is done. Most codes in C program needs a semicolon to denote where the line ends.

The command getchar() informs the compiler to stop once it reaches the end of the function and standby for an input from the keyboard before continuing. This command is very useful because most compilers would run the C program and then immediately exits the window. The getchar() command would prevent the compiler to close the window until after a keystroke .is made.

The command return 0 denotes that the function has ended. For this particular C program, it started as an int, which indicates that the program has to return an integer once it is done running. The "0" is an indication that the compiler ran the program correctly. If another number is returned at the end of the program, it means that there was an error somewhere in the program.

Compiling the program

To compile the program, type the code into the program's code editor. Save this as a type of *.c file, then click the Run or Build button.

Commenting on the code

Any comments placed on codes are not compiled. These allow the user to give details on what happens in the function. Comments are good reminders on what the code is all about and for what. Comments also help other developers to understand what the code when they look at it.

To make a comment, add a /* at the beginning of the comment. End the written comment with a */. When commenting, comment on everything except the basic portions of the code, where explanations are no longer necessary because the meanings are already clearly understood.

Also, comments can be utilized for quick removal of code parts without having to delete them. Just enclose portions of the code in /* */, then compile. Remove these tags if these portions are to be added back into the code.

USING VARIABLES

Understanding variables

Define the variables before using them. Some common ones include char, float and int.

Declaring variables

Again, variables have to be declared before the program can use them. To declare, enter data type and then the name of the variable. Take a look at these examples:

```
char name;
```

float x;

int f, g, i, j;

Multiple variables can also be declared all on a single line, on condition that all of them belong to the same data type. Just separate the names of the variables commas (i.e., int f, g, i, j;).

When declaring variables, always end the line with a semicolon to denote that the line has ended.

Location on declaring the variables

Declaring variables is done at the start of the code block. This is the portion of the code enclosed by the brackets {}. The program won't function well if variables are declared later within the code block.

Variables for storing user input

Simple programs can be written using variables. These programs will store inputs of the user. Simple programs will use the function scanf, which searches the user's input for particular values. Take a look at this example:

```
#include <stdio.h>

int main()
{
    int x;

    printf( "45: " );
    scanf( "%d", &x );
    printf( "45 %d", x );
    getchar();
    return 0;
}
```

The string &d informs the function scanf to search the input for any integers.

The command & placed before the x variable informs the function scanf where it can search for the specific variable so that the function can change it. It also informs the function to store the defined integer within the variable.

The last printf tells the compiler to read back the integer input into the screen as a feedback for the user to check.

Manipulating variables

Mathematical expressions can be used, which allow users to manipulate stored variables. When using mathematical expressions, it is most important to remember to use the "=" distinction. A single = will set the variable's value. A == (double equal sign) is placed when the goal is to compare the values on both sides of the sign, to check if the values are equal.

For example:

x = 2 * 4; /* sets the value of "x" to 2 * 4, or 8 */

x = x + 8; /* adds 8 to the original "x " value, and defines the new "x" value as the specific variable */

x == 18; /* determines if the value of "x" is equal to 18 */

x < 11; /* determines if the "x" value is lower than 11 */

CONDITIONAL STATEMENTS

Conditional statements can also be used within the C program. In fact, most programs are driven by these statements. These are determined as either False or True and then acted upon depending on the results. The most widely used and basic conditional statement is if.

In C, False and True statements are treated differently. Statements that are "TRUE" are those that end up equal to nonzero numbers. For example, when a comparison is performed, the outcome is a "TRUE" statement if the returned numerical value is "1". The result is a "FALSE" statement if the value that returns is "0".

Basic conditional operators

The operation of conditional statements is based on mathematical operators used in comparing values. The most common conditional operators include the following:

   < /* less than */

6 < 15 TRUE

   > /* greater than */

10 > 5 TRUE

<= /* less than or equal to */

4 <= 8 TRUE

>= /* greater than or equal to */

8 >= 8 TRUE

!= /* not equal to */

4 != 5 TRUE

== /* equal to */

7 == 7 TRUE

How to write a basic "IF" conditional statement

A conditional "IF" statement is used in determining what the next step in the program is after evaluation of the statement. These can be combined with other types of conditional statements in order to create multiple and powerful options.

Take a look at this example:

```c
#include <stdio.h>

int main()
{
if ( 4 < 7 )
    printf( "4 is less than 7");
    getchar();
}
```

The "ELSE/ELSE IF" statements

These statements can be used in expanding the conditional statements. Build upon the "IF" statements with "ELSE" and "ELSE IF" type of conditional statements, which will handle different types of results. An "ELSE" statement will be run when the IF statement result is FALSE. An "ELSE IF" statement will allow for the inclusion of multiple IF statements in one code block, which will handle all the various cases of the statement.

Take a look at this example:

```c
#include <stdio.h>


int main()
{
 int age;

 printf( "Please type current age: " );
 scanf( "%d", &age );
 if ( age <= 10 ) {
  printf( "You are just a kid!\n" );
 }
 else if ( age < 30 ) {
  printf( "Being a young adult is pretty awesome!\n" );
 }
 else if ( age < 50 ) {
  printf( "You are young at heart!\n" );
 }
 else {
  printf( "Age comes with wisdom.\n" );
 }
 return 0;
}
```

The above program will take all the input from the user and will run it through the different defined IF statements. If the input (number) satisfies the 1st IF statement, the 1st printf statement will be returned. If it does not, then input will be run through each of the "ELSE IF" statements until a match is found. If after all the "ELSE IF" statements have been run and nothing works, the input will be run through the "ELSE" statement at the last part of the program.

LOOPS

Loops are among the most important parts of C programming. These allow the user to repeat code blocks until particular conditions have been met. Loops make implementing repeated actions easy and reduce the need to write new conditional statements each time.

There are 3 main types of loops in C programming. These are FOR, WHILE and Do... WHILE.

"FOR" Loop

The "FOR" loop is the most useful and commonly used type of loop in C programming. This loop continues to run the function until the conditions set for this loop are met. There are 3 conditions required by the FOR loop. These include initialization of the variable, meeting the condition and how updating of the variable is done. All of these conditions need not be met at the same time, but a blank space with semicolon is still needed to prevent the loop from running continuously.

Take a look at this example:

```
#include <stdio.h>

int main()
{
int y;

for ( y = 0; y < 10; y++;){
  printf( "%d\n", y );
}
getchar();
}
```

The value of y has been set to 0, and the loop is programmed to continue running as long as the y value remains less than 10. At each run (loop), the y value is increased by 1 before the loop is repeated. Hence, once the value of y is equivalent to 10 (after 10 loops), the above loop will then break.

WHILE Loop

These are simpler than the FOR loops. There is only one condition, which is that as long as the condition remains TRUE, the loop continues to run. Variables need not to be initialized or updated, but can be done within the loop's main body.

Take a look at this example:

```
#include <stdio.h>

int main()
{
int y;

while ( y <= 20 ){
printf( "%d\n", y );
y++;
}
getchar();
}
```

In the above program, the command y++ will add 1 to the variable y for each execution of the loop. When the value of y reaches 21, the loop will break.

DO...WHILE Loop

This is a very useful loop to ensure at least 1 run. FOR and WHILE loops check the conditions at the start of the loop, which ensures that it could not immediately pass and fail. DO...WHILE loops will check the conditions when the loop is finished. This ensures that the loop will run at last once before a pass and fail occurs.

Take a look at this example:

```
#include <stdio.h>

int main()
{
int y;
```

```
y = 10;

do {

    printf("This loop is running!\n");

} while ( y != 10 );

getchar();

}
```

This type of loop displays the message whether the condition results turn out TRUE or FALSE. The *y* variable is set to 10. The WHILE loop has been set to run when the *y* value is not equal to 10, at which the loop ends. The message was printed because the condition is not checked until the loop has ended.

The WHILE portion of the DO..WHILE loop must end with a semicolon. This is also the only instance when a loop ends this way.

Conclusion

Thank you again for purchasing this book!

I hope this book was able to help you to understand the complex terms and language used in C. this programming method can put off a lot of users because of its seemingly complexity. However, with the right basic knowledge, soon, you will be programming more complex things with C.

The next step is to start executing these examples. Reading and understanding this book is not enough, although this will push you into the right direction. Execution will cement the knowledge and give you the skill and deeper understanding of C.

Finally, if you enjoyed this book, please take the time to share your thoughts and post a review on Amazon. We do our best to reach out to readers and provide the best value we can. Your positive review will help us achieve that. It'd be greatly appreciated!

Thank you and good luck!

Check Out My Other Books

Below you'll find some of my other popular books that are popular on Amazon and Kindle as well. Simply click on the links below to check them out. Alternatively, you can visit my author page on Amazon to see other work done by me.

C Programming Success in a Day

Android Programming in a Day

C ++ Programming Success in a Day

Python Programming in a Day

PHP Programming Professional Made Easy

HTML Professional Programming Made Easy

JavaScript Programming Made Easy

CSS Programming Professional Made Easy

Windows 8 Tips for Beginners

If the links do not work, for whatever reason, you can simply search for these titles on the Amazon website to find them.

www.ingramcontent.com/pod-product-compliance
Lightning Source LLC
Chambersburg PA
CBHW061025050326
40689CB00012B/2706